My toys have
shapes

Bobbie Kalman

 Crabtree Publishing Company

www.crabtreebooks.com

Created by Bobbie Kalman

Author and Editor-in-Chief
Bobbie Kalman

Educational consultants
Elaine Hurst
Joan King
Reagan Miller

Editors
Reagan Miller
Joan King
Kathy Middleton

Proofreader
Crystal Sikkens

Design
Bobbie Kalman
Katherine Berti

Photo research
Bobbie Kalman

Production coordinator
Katherine Berti

Prepress technician
Katherine Berti

Shape illustrations by Katherine Berti
Photographs by Shutterstock

Library and Archives Canada Cataloguing in Publication

Kalman, Bobbie, 1947-
    My toys have shapes / Bobbie Kalman.

(My world)
ISBN 978-0-7787-9413-4 (bound).--ISBN 978-0-7787-9457-8 (pbk.)

    1. Shapes--Juvenile literature. 2. Geometry--Juvenile literature.
3. Toys--Juvenile literature. I. Title. II. Series: My world (St. Catharines, Ont.)

QA445.5.K335 2010   j516'.1   C2009-906049-3

Library of Congress Cataloging-in-Publication Data

Kalman, Bobbie.
My toys have shapes / Bobbie Kalman.
    p. cm. -- (My world)
ISBN 978-0-7787-9413-4 (reinforced lib. bdg. : alk. paper) -- ISBN 978-0-7787-9457-8 (pbk. : alk. paper)
1. Geometry--Juvenile literature. 2. Shapes--Juvenile literature. I. Title.
II. Series.

QA445.5. K349 2010
516'.15--dc22

                                                2009040951

Crabtree Publishing Company

www.crabtreebooks.com   1-800-387-7650

Printed in China/122009/CT20091009

Published in Canada
Crabtree Publishing
616 Welland Ave.
St. Catharines, Ontario
L2M 5V6

Published in the United States
Crabtree Publishing
PMB 59051
350 Fifth Avenue, 59th Floor
New York, New York 10118

Published in the United Kingdom
Crabtree Publishing
Maritime House
Basin Road North, Hove
BN41 1WR

Published in Australia
Crabtree Publishing
386 Mt. Alexander Rd.
Ascot Vale (Melbourne)
VIC 3032

Words to know

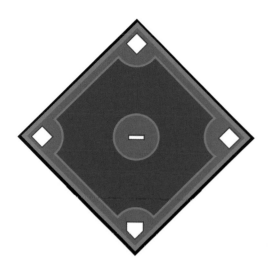

baseball field

blocks

football

sign

soccer ball

toy house

3

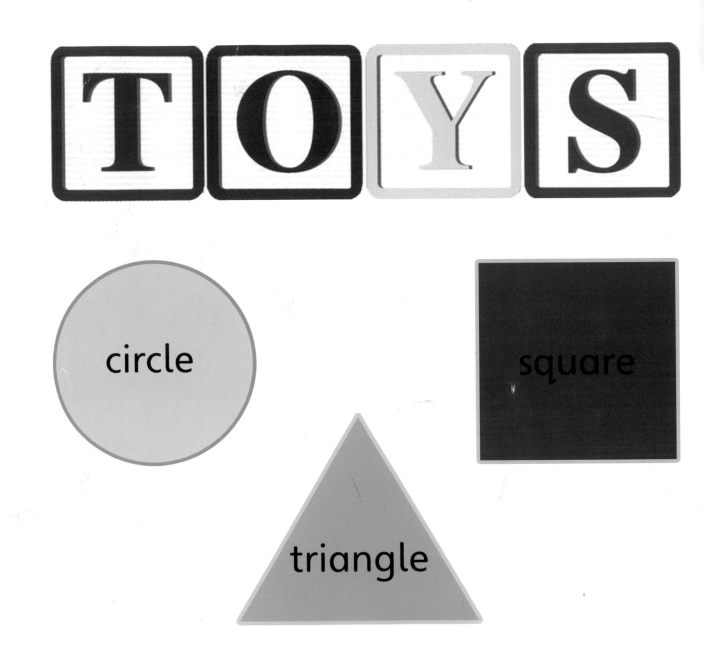

TOYS

circle

square

triangle

My toys have shapes.

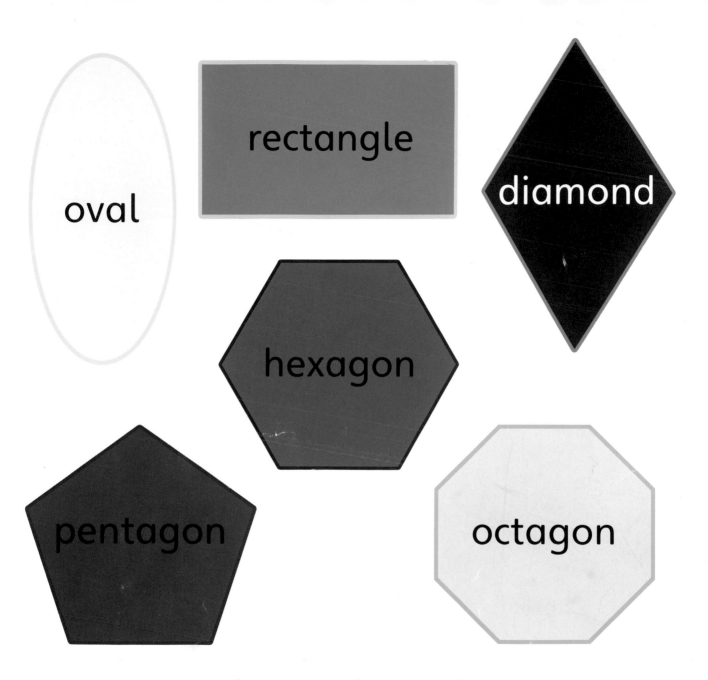

oval

rectangle

diamond

hexagon

pentagon

octagon

Do you know these shapes?

circle

My ball has a circle shape.

oval

My football has an oval shape.

square

My blocks have a square shape.

rectangle

My blocks have a rectangle shape.

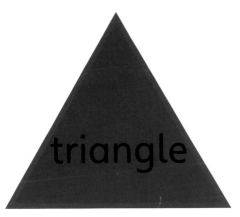

triangle

My toy house has a triangle shape.

My baseball field has a diamond shape.

11

pentagon

My soccer ball has **pentagon** shapes.

hexagon

My soccer ball has hexagon shapes.

octagon

A stop sign has an octagon shape.

What shapes can you find?

Notes for adults

Outlines and shapes

Many toys have more than one shape. A child's toy house may be mostly square or rectangular, but it has triangles, as well. The outline of a soccer ball is round, but the ball's pattern also has two other shapes—pentagons and hexagons. The white hexagons are hard to see in white-and-black soccer balls because they are like space holders between the black pentagons. The hexagons are much more visible in colorful soccer balls. Ask children to name some outline shapes they see in their toys and then look for other shapes in or on the toys.

Shape pictures

Use construction paper to cut out the shapes shown in this book. Ask the children to use the shapes to create pictures, such as animals, bugs, or cars. Children will begin to see the different shapes within the main shapes of objects. How many objects can they make using squares, rectangles, ovals, circles, diamonds, pentagons, hexagons, and octagons?

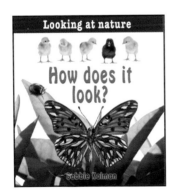

Patterns are made up of colors and shapes, such as spots, stripes, and circles. Patterns create camouflage in nature. Children can explore the use of patterns in **How does it look?**
Guided Reading: J

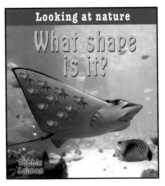

What shape is it? *shows the amazing shapes found in nature, such as triangles in the wings of butterflies and circles and spheres in the shapes of the Earth, moon, and sun.*
Guided Reading: I